YOUNG ENTREPRENEURS: TIPS AND TRICKS FOR SUCCESS

YOUNG

ENTREPRENEURS

TIPS AND TRICKS FOR

SUCCESS

YOUNG ENTREPRENEURS: TIPS AND TRICKS FOR SUCCESS

INDEX

How much do we need to produce?

Myths about entrepreneurship

Business Ethics

Communication tips for business management

Time management for business owners

Leadership attributes for business success

Calculate your initial costs

Obtaining investment funds for your company

Brand your business

Entrepreneurship: a visión

So far you've read some of the features of entrepreneurship. "Practice makes perfect" is the motto of everything in life and especially if you own a business. The knowledge embodied in books can help you avoid mistakes, but nothing is better than the practical experience of seeing what works for you.

You have the right passion, the right business format and all the skills. But before you take the leap of faith; be sure to be prepared in other aspects as well.

From the beginning of the business to running smoothly requires a lot of dedication and sacrifice. Which means that personal life, young or old, will take a few blows? Family and friends should be supportive, knowing what it takes to start a business and its effect on family life. Many of you may choose to have a job in the early days of starting a business; this means that all of your free time has to be devoted to running the business.

Entrepreneurship will affect your health. Being thin and mean is good for business, but that often means spending more hours doing what you would pay other people to do. Therefore, to survive those more than 14 hours of work a day, seven days a week you must be at the peak of your physical and mental condition. Proper nutrition and a regular exercise regimen will take care of

your health. It's hard to enjoy success lying in a hospital bed.

Know your strengths in the business and hire others to do the other jobs. Many homeowners think they should be good at everything. That's probably not the case. Although sometimes knowing all aspects of the business is advantageous. Just in case someone gets sick. From a business point of view, having a team in which you are the weakest link is not bad.

In addition to knowing your strengths, you should also know your comfort zones.

Do you feel comfortable being the boss and having employees who are older than you?

Dealing with the multiple personalities your employees possess?

Handle money and make financial decisions? Start getting into debt first by starting the business before you see the profits?

Leave a few years before you see enough profit to get a fixed paycheck?

These are just a few things to keep in mind and have a backup plan or two ready in case you run into them along the way.

Become an entrepreneur

To become a successful entrepreneur you need good ideas, a little luck, money and a lot of work. 90% of successful people fail, which means that to earn something (profits, equity, etc.) you must first lose something (your initial investment). Phat-farm is a multi-million dollar company whose owner Russell Simmons lost 10 million dollars in the first five years.

It doesn't require much experience and resources, but to become a successful entrepreneur you need passion and persistence.

Turning everyday ideas into business is what makes an ordinary entrepreneur extraordinary. This talent or gift is what makes them unique. Most start with very limited resources and outpace their competitors through personal effort. Moves have to be fast and good decisions have to be made to gain market share and advance in the case of great competitors.

They differ in age, sex and race, but it is easy to recognize an entrepreneur and his business. They can be enriched by their ideas, but the starting point is to look for areas that are not being addressed and change the way things are done. A good idea is not the same as an ideal opportunity. Understanding the distinction will save you time, effort and money.

The entrepreneur creates a vision and pushes the company through ups and downs toward fulfilling that vision. Becoming an entrepreneur is at the same time frightening, exciting, and worrisome and yet an exciting experience. But before you become one, you must first understand the concept of entrepreneurship. There are many types of entrepreneurs, such as social, domiciliary, virtual, traditional, etc.

The widely accepted definition of entrepreneurship would be to create a new organization or take over an old one to respond to certain identified opportunities. You should be aware that a large number of new businesses fail. The most successful people are those who are not afraid to experiment, learn from their past mistakes and rectify to succeed.

The difference between an entrepreneur and a small business owner is the process or method you want to instill for business expansion. Small business owners would like their business to be as it is, i.e. small and geographically limited, earning only a few million in its entire useful life.

Entrepreneurial companies seek to make millions in the first 3-5 years and expand internationally using all opportunities. Other characteristics would be concentration, an inclination to innovation and the creation of new values to shake up the market. In the United States, small businesses provide the maximum number of jobs, while entrepreneurs provide most of the workforce.

Use Your Youth Advantage

Now you're just a kid, concentrate on your studies. Business requires experience. Blah blah blah blah blah.... People will have numerous reasons not to start a business, all for good intentions.

But before you swallow all that, think for a moment about Bill Gates who left Harvard to start Microsoft, Michael Dell who left the University of Texas to start Dell, Milton Hershey who opened his first candy store when he was 18, Fred Smith who, while attending Yale, received a "C" in his Fedex business plan and decided to start his business anyway, Steve Jobs who left Reed

University to start Apple, William Hewlett and David Packard who started HP out of a garage after graduating from Stanford or the thousands of young people who have started a business and have been successful.

What would have happened if they had been convinced of these unconvincing arguments and backed up by their business plan? We will have to live without a Dell, a Microsoft, an HP, a Hersheys, a Fedex or an Apple... oh! Horrible horror!

The best way to tilt the card in your favor:

Adults expect less from young people and can be used to their advantage. It's okay if you're not perfectly polished. It will take less

effort to please customers and make a name for yourself in the media.

There is little competition from other students, which makes your story more worthy of press, scholarships, competition, customers and awards.

There are many nonprofits and individuals who support youth efforts. The first on this list is your school, which probably has teachers who have contacts in the business community who can help you.

Students often have income from their parents. Even if it's not consistent, then it's something you know you can always look for. If your adventure fails when you're

young, you definitely won't starve or lose your home.

The practical knowledge you learn by running your business can help your academic work and vice versa. Some schools will allow you to earn academic credit from an independent study of your business. You can also base class projects on your business.

Young people have a new perspective on the world. This perspective helps them see many opportunities that until now had not been exploited. The founders of Microsoft, Dell, HP, Hersheys, Apple and Forex will vouch for you.

Strategic Thinking for Young Entrepreneurs

Strategic thinking is both science and art form. You need to use both the right and left sides of your brain to really excel, and this requires confidence and practice.

The following are some of the skills that great strategists possess and use on a daily basis:

They see great things and then use strategic thinking to make them a reality. Having these two skills means they can see a desirable future and develop a strategy that focuses on details and the big picture in order to create it.

Take time off the daily hassles of a 9 to 5 year job. All great strategists do this. Simply go to a quiet place - preferably a weekend retreat, but a day or even an afternoon off, if not - and sit down with your hat on to think. Try it.

Strategic thinking, as its name suggests, is not about making quick money, but about looking at the big picture and planning for years to come. Immediate results may not be impressive, but in the long run, strategic thinking pays off. One of the reasons for the unimpressive immediate result is that strategies, like masterpieces, take time to create, fine-tune, and revise.

All true strategists are fully aware of everything that happens around them. In all business matters, there are clues, whether subtle or otherwise, that alert those who notice them of the possible directions in which concern may be taken. As the great strategists absorb this information, it helps them better formulate their plans when inspiration arrives, whether on vacation, during a morning walk or just after the first cup of espresso. Their ability to detect and create bonds keeps them in good standing.

Make sure your big idea isn't a chimera. All great thinkers must make sure that their idea is valid, that it stays in a world full of problems and changes. You need to constantly review and fine-tune your plans.

Use the experiences you've had to help you

plan better. If a shortcut has worked before and saved you a lot of time and effort, don't hesitate to adapt it to a new plan.

Don't just depend on yourself, no matter how good you think and/or know you are. Use reliable colleagues to bounce off your ideas. In the case of strategic thinking, "two heads are better than one" is a truer adage that "too many cooks spoil the broth.

Create a successful small business marketing plan in 7 easy steps

Before starting a small business, first understand the need of the target market and then try to provide a suitable solution.

These 7 steps should be used by entrepreneurs who want to start a new business or create a marketing plan for an existing successful installation. Most people talk about the greatness of their products or services. Instead, you should regularly educate the target market and build a relationship of trust and credibility.

"Think marketing is the mindset to develop for your products and services. You have to sell constantly. Don't be fooled by stop and go marketing. Some small entrepreneurs start marketing only during low seasons.

Having a successful marketing plan is essential for entrepreneurship. Profits and growth are directly proportional to effective marketing.

If you're thinking about where to start, this 7-step guide will help you understand the market and the business.

We will answer the following questions:

1. Who is your target market? Who is your ideal customer? What research is needed to learn more about the target market?

2. What does your ideal customer want? What do your products and services do for them? What problems your customer has are solved by your product? What solutions does your customer need? What is your USP that makes it unique? What are the industry trends? What will make your customer react? What do you sell? (For example, are you selling eyeglasses or vision?) What is your brand of products and services? What would be the price?

3. Where is your ideal customer? Geographically, where are they? Where will

they be positioned to easily reach them? Where will they get their marketing messages from? Will you review personal conversations, organize seminars or write a blog, newsletter or article?

4. When...? How frequent will your marketing messages be? When are your customers most likely to buy?

5. Why...? Why are you in business? Why do customers come to you? Why shouldn't they go to their competitors and choose their products?

6. How... how does your customer buy? How will you reach potential customers? How will you communicate your marketing strategies?

How will you provide information to your customers so they can make the purchase decision?

7. Marketing Mentality - Try to master a marketing mentality and your small business will move toward profits and success.

The Key Factors of a Successful Entrepreneurship

Starting a business involves some significant changes in the life of the entrepreneur:

1) Permanent financial freedom.

2) Flexibility of schedules.

3) The satisfaction of making one's life come true - regardless of making the business grow into a gigantic structure or just keep doing what you like to do and make a living.

In addition to the excitement of new ventures, comes the challenge of wearing too many hats: strategic planning, marketing, sales, production, customer service, accounting, and financing. Even if the business is small, the tasks are enormous.

Whatever the field, the main factors of a successful venture remain the same.

1) A good idea.

2) An effective marketing plan that is not too expensive.

3) Efficient operation.

Ideas for the future

The right business idea is crucial to the
success of the company. First, you must be
passionate about the work area. Secondly,
you must possess sufficient knowledge,
talent and experience to move forward.
Finally, choose a business that produces
small, stable income without large
investments. This will eventually support
you and your family. Some ideas that can be
considered are: independent writing, online
marketing, web design, accounting, etc.

Promotion

The basic tool to market your products and services would be the distribution of business cards. You can design the card yourself using different business card templates, but it would be wiser to spend some money and let a professional do it. Only $20 will give you 500 cards.

Color cards are a little more expensive. The next step is to build a website that allows prospects to see the information 24 hours a day, 365 days a year. About $50 is the annual cost of maintaining the website.

Another 80 dollars more would give you two simple web pages. If Internet prospects look

good, then spend $50 on online pay-per-click (PPC) ads. $50 on PPC will bring you more customers and also generate revenue.

Operational Efficiency

Business management (marketing, sales, production, etc.) takes all the time away from small business owners. They do not have the time (or knowledge) to plan business expansion. The result is that either they remain a small business, or they disappear if there is a drastic change in the market.

Operation efficiency is even more necessary in smaller companies than in established farms.

Some methods to improve the efficiency of the operation.

1) Streamline business processes.

2) Use productivity software.

3) Outsourcing and other services.

Something like - hiring an accountant for tax returns and accounting, a collection agency for debt collection, etc. must be done. Always take the time to expand your business.

Mistakes in the creation of companies

An economy is made up mainly of producers and consumers, who are engaged in what is known as a transaction. An economic transaction would be the transfer of goods and services from producers to consumers in exchange for money.

The creation of goods involves several activities. These activities can be collectively referred to as a business or an enterprise. Starting a business is neither easy nor quick. Here are some essential elements that are required to do the same.

What to produce?

There are many goods that make up an economy. Therefore, the producer must decide which of them to produce. The search for one's own profit cannot be the only criterion. Resources are scarce and must be used optimally and for the welfare of society.

How to produce?

There can be many methods of producing a commodity. Therefore, the producer must opt for a process that fully exploits resources at minimal cost.

How much do we need to produce?

An oversupply will lower the price and the producers will eventually suffer a loss. Therefore, produce to meet market demand.

Capital

To start a business it is necessary to have enough investment power. If a producer does not have the necessary capital, he can obtain loans from financial institutions or partner with other investors to obtain support for collective investment.

Market research

It is not enough to have money to create a company. You have to understand the consumption pattern of the market. Even if the product has a high probability of sale, it must be marketed in a way that attracts the attention of the buyer. Otherwise, consumers may not know all the details of the product.

Scale of production

Normally, a company cannot achieve the optimal level of production in the short term. This is due to fixed production inputs that cannot be changed according to needs. These inputs give rise to fixed costs that reduce the producer's income. However, over time, as the business reaches a considerable scale, these fixed inputs disappear and only the variables remain, i.e. the producer faces a variable cost.

Delegation of activities

No business can be sustained on the basis of a single show. There are too many activities involved. Therefore, it is cheaper, more efficient and necessary to delegate functions to people specialized in those fields.

Therefore, violation of any of the above guidelines is a mistake for which the company suffers.

Myths about entrepreneurship

There are many myths about being an entrepreneur, most of which have been created by the media.

While some are true, others are clearly false. The following are the five most important myths:

Myth 1: Entrepreneurs want money. Period.

Many people think that entrepreneurs are in this just for the money. This is true to a certain extent: fear of poverty, or simply financial insecurity, could well lead anyone to higher heights, and there are those who do it for the money, but for most people, the money is not the whole and the whole.

Many entrepreneurs have ego and/or emotion as their main motives, many do not maintain the luxurious lifestyles expected of them, and most consider money as a way of keeping score.

Myth 2: My gain, your loss.

People often refer to success in business at someone else's expense. What they mean, obviously, is that if an entrepreneur is winning, someone somewhere has paid the

price. This makes it seem like there has to be a winner and a loser in every business. This is sometimes called the "zero-sum game".

Actually, entrepreneurs are creative thinkers. Instead of playing for a "zero-sum" result, and contrary to popular assumption, they often try to reach a compromise that means everyone leaves the table satisfied.

Myth 3: The greater the risk, the greater the reward.

Many young businessmen, having heard this, accept it as a Gospel truth.

The relationship between risk and reward is

complicated and in no way reducible to a simple statement.

Risks in business are not the same as jumping off a cliff in the dark: knowledge, experience, wisdom, hard work and perseverance modify both `risk' and `reward.

Myth 4: Entrepreneurs get rich fast.

The rise of dotcom millionaires definitely makes entrepreneurs look like they are making quick money, but you must remember that nothing is as easy as it seems.

You may think that entrepreneurs get rich extremely fast, but a lot of work goes into

44

developing the ideas/products that make them rich.

Myth 5: A good business plan is the entrepreneur's critical path to success.

This is more true than most other myths, since you are unlikely to be granted loans without a solid business plan. However, a loan does not in any way equate to good money.

Business plans are guidelines, yes, but to be successful, much more is needed.

Business Ethics

"Honesty is the best policy," a phrase that is valid not only in everyday life, but also in business ethics.

Ethics is very important for all entrepreneurs. However, many neglect ethics as an important concept that has a great impact on a person's success as an entrepreneur and investor. Business, after all, involves dealing with money, whether owned or borrowed.

It also involves building successful, money-based relationships with customers and clients. These relationships must be built on trust, and having an ethical foundation is imperative to building trust. Therefore, ethics is the cornerstone of business success.

It is important to realize that ethics is important regardless of the size of the company. Whether your company is large or small, or your customers are many or few, the importance of adhering to high ethical standards is the same.

Business ethics is closely linked to the moral value chain that is intertwined throughout your operations. Moral value affects each and every customer. There can be no exceptions regardless of whether your customers are 10 or 10,000 or more. Ethics applies to each and every one of them.

As a discipline, business ethics can be applied or theoretical. Or to put it another way, it can be pragmatic or philosophical. The former typically evolves into the do's and don'ts, acting as a guide to ethical behavior. These latter studies involve probing the whys and wherefores of ethics in business. It also examines the question of the definition of ethics.

It promotes high standards, develops a code and helps the entrepreneur to self-assess his or her own personal ethical standard. This standard, in turn, helps the company to enunciate the standards of ethical behaviour of its employees. An honest business employs only honest professionals. This must be clearly understood in the future.

In most successful business organizations, high ethical standards are mandatory. An employee, who bribes someone, even in the interests of his or her employer, is likely to be fired. Many multinationals refuse to do business in countries where bribes are commonly given and accepted. These are examples of the applied side of business ethics.

One last point... In some factors there can be no ethical compromises, regardless of profit or loss considerations. For example, under no circumstances should a company violate the laws of the country in which it is in business, whether it likes these laws or not.

Communication tips for business management

Even if you have brilliant ideas, they're worthless unless you share them. Therefore, being able to communicate effectively is just as important as being able to come up with great ideas. However, not everyone is good at communication, and they need practice to be able to do so.

Suppose that a situation arises in which, for external reasons, it is necessary to immediately double the company's production. But their managers cannot do the work for the employees, who are not willing to make an extra effort for the company. This results in the loss of both money and reputation for the company.

So what's the problem? It's not that employees aren't paid or deprived of other benefits. So the real problem here is the lack of communication between employer and employee.

It is often forgotten that internal communication is an integral part of the business communication strategy. The whole focus being on external communication, the firm and its managers cheerfully paint pink pictures for customers. This leads to a strong marketing side, no doubt, but rather weakens the operational strategy.

Another problem caused by bad communication and/or lack of communication is the growth of the negative vine. This unofficial channel of communication can lead to disaffection, causing profits to decrease.

To ensure growth, it is necessary to have both internal and external communication channels. The entire communication system must be one piece and purpose. It cannot be allowed to speak plainly. Everything that is communicated, whether to customers or employees, must be carefully crafted in order to achieve the goals that have been set.

If you focus on the needs of your target segment, you can probably establish an effective communication strategy. They care about their objectives, but only to the extent that they benefit from it. So identify with their needs and communicate their objectives in terms they identify with.

If you welcome suggestions and encourage your employees to comment, they will have the opportunity to present their suggestions constructively, but this will also suppress the rumour and allow them to feel involved.

When you receive comments or suggestions, react positively. Assure your employees that their complaints are being noted and that positive actions will be taken.

Make sure your message does not get lost in a maze of jargon and can be understood by

YOUNG ENTREPRENEURS: TIPS AND TRICKS FOR SUCCESS

your target audience.

In short, to achieve your objectives, you must communicate your ideas clearly.

Time management for business owners

Time management is considered as the art that teaches you the various techniques to increase your efficiency and complete the work pending. It is important to be able to control and manage time in your personal life, but in the case of your business, it is critical and necessary to achieve success.

Time management programs help small business owners manage and control time effectively through the use of electronic calendars and schedulers. The "to-do list" has proven to be an effective time management tool. Scheduling actions, however, is also

time consuming, making the use of software an essential necessity.

Success is the result of planning your objectives as well as your time, implementing routines and scheduling tasks. Time management programs can reinforce employees' workflow and production activities using written or electronic reminders or "to do list" software.

It is imperative that small business owners plan, prepare, prioritize and control their activities along with the activities of other team members, and also set goals for the success of the business.

This is really an easy task once you have the

right time management software. Many of these programs include short- and long-term goal planning, data analysis, future predictions and performance charts. These are features that are not available in the basic software task list. Don't underestimate the importance of "to-do" software when planning your business activities or setting your goals.

Time management is extremely important for a small business. Therefore, time management gurus are common today who give advice on how to manage their time. They are better known as time managers, who after reading your business plan; prioritize activities for work teams on a daily basis.

With the help of time management software, they can provide entrepreneurs with detailed reports of daily activity trends, allowing them to rectify values, activities and priorities.

Time managers are also the common name given to time management programs and to the different time management solutions available in today's market for small businesses. These range from classic paper books, to various task list software, organizers, reminders, calendars and planners, among many other things.

Leadership attributes for business success

Leadership qualities are not something you are born with and therefore need to be acquired if you are an aspiring entrepreneur. Skills can be easily acquired if you take into account some basic things that are necessary for any type of leadership, whether in business or otherwise. The success of any business depends on the efficiency of the manager or owner in building a healthy and productive work culture.

Any leader must have a vision for the work he or she is managing. It is important to have the right kind of vision, as this is extremely crucial to keeping the various aspects of the job together. A wrong vision will not only lead employees astray, it will also ruin the whole business. A clear vision will help you get started and will also help you see the job successfully.

A vision is something for which the whole company works and keeps it going until it is achieved.

Effective entrepreneurship will help the manager and his or her employees realize this vision. Ideas and opinions should be shared from all points of view. This would make everyone feel part of the whole company. The manager must ensure that his or her employees are not merely qualified workers who are there just to make money,

but are committed to the company's vision.

The manager must inspire and motivate employees to work toward a common goal. The business would then become a means to achieve these goals. This does not mean that the focus should be exclusively on results and not on the work itself. Each step taken by employees must be carefully analyzed and employees must receive feedback on the progress of the work.

This would ensure the quality of the experts as well as commendable results for the company. The leader must create a healthy work environment that gives employees the space and freedom to think freely and apply their imagination to get the job done. A rigid work system would alienate employees from each other and from the leader. This would jeopardize the whole system and affect the vision of the company.

Any type of business includes the target audience, who are the company's customers. The leader must also focus on the customers, getting results that reach a wider audience.

Calculate your initial costs

Start-up costs pose problems for all of us. They are instrumental in getting one in an arrangement and therefore the measurement of their stakes is very important. So here are ten beneficial tips on how to estimate the start-up costs of your business.

1. First, you need to think carefully and include the costs of all the things you need in estimating the start-up costs of your business. Always remember, that this amount is different from the basic amount of cost required for your business to survive during the year. In addition to this, there are other things that need money and that include advertisements, office chairs and supplies, inventory, cash registers and service supplies. The initial cost should also take into account any other items you have forgotten.

2. Don't take bank loans unless absolutely necessary. And even if you make sure you can pay the interest the bank is going to charge. Also ask about interest rates, you don't want them to be too high.

3. Consider your household expenses during the period that is the start time of your business. Make sure you have enough cash to cover the amount or the credentials to purchase a loan that covers the amount.

4. You should be able to judge how much

money is required for your business to survive its first year. You also need to be prepared for any other sporadic expenses that may occur from time to time during that year.

5. Organize yourself so that you are prepared for any additional costs that may arise intermittently throughout the year.

6. Consider year-round food expenses. Your budget should leave enough money for food and other basic expenses. This will protect you from risks during the first year of business.

7. Your company requires credentials that will secure a loan in case your money runs out at some point during the year. It is advisable that you get a loan only if you can generate enough sales to repay the loan. If your business doesn't go very well during the first year, you may want to close it.

8. The salary you have to pay your employees, that is, if you have employees, is something else to keep in mind. This includes commercial insurance, any health insurance and, of course, workers' payments. You also have to pay an extra charge to the city for any part-time or full-time employees you have working for your company.

9. You may have to take exams to get certified depending on the nature of the business you are starting. These tests cost money. In addition, you have to be aware of any other rules or regulations that your type of business involves.

10. You can always sell some personal belongings to get extra money if you don't have enough. But make sure your business offers enough security to sell these items. The last thing you want is to end up ruined by losing your company and also all your expensive belongings because you sold them so you had enough money to start the company.

Obtaining investment funds for your company

Successful businessmen and women who want to invest their capital in struggling businesses or in franchising are called Business Angels. In return for the investment, they usually want convertible debt or equity ownership. In order to get a good return on their investment, they plan to use their experience to turn businesses into successes.

Because of their experience, Business Angels are very careful about who they invest in. Their action plan is to invest when stocks are cheap, work with the company, build it and then sell the mature company after a few

years to other brokers or the original owner.

Dragons Den is a popular program that has investors waiting to invest in a business. As a business owner, it is important to have a good sales pitch and prepare ahead of time. It helps to have a clear business strategy. Dragons are often good at realizing if the target audience and market have not been properly researched.

To impress dragons, it is important to have accurate sales projections - they want facts as answers to their questions, not lies. Generally, they will not invest in a high-risk business if they believe it is possible. They are experts in their field, so their advice on business ideas is very valuable and should be taken into account.

Trust is very important. Voice, posture and attitude are very revealing when it comes to trust, so it helps to have these areas covered when convincing potential investors. Questions should be prepared for: thinking about what investors might ask is a good strategy.

Questions about potential profits and company revenues are natural, so the key is to think differently. Areas of the business that make it unique and different from others should be highlighted in order to eliminate competition.

Commitment is another vital factor. Business angels like to see engaged workers. They are usually impressed if the company includes part of the beginner's equity. However, if thousands of pounds have already been invested in the business and it is still not making money, they will be cautious.

Business Angels are now very easy to find, thanks to the Internet. There are hundreds of sites dedicated to finding the right investor for a business. There are also groups of angels or networks of angels. So starting a business has never been easier - investment is child's play!

Brand your business

Tying an identifiable brand to your business is very important to ensure the success of your business. The term Branding is a conglomerate of numerous functions that must be assumed to ensure the success of the business. Branding initiates subsequent actions in various areas, such as:

1. Increase the perception and visibility of the name and logo of the company.

2. Formulate a company name that can immediately inspire public faith.

3. Carefully identify and nurture the profile of the potential consumer.

The brand, including the company name and logo, is not a tangible asset of a company, unlike physical assets such as resources and institutions, and is only useful to increase the goodwill of the company and accentuate the reputation and identity of the company.

Careful and cautious planning must go into branding before it is implemented to maximize profits. Identifying and isolating the consumer attraction base with specific incentives and understanding of their requirements must be ensured before branding is undertaken.

Some essential steps to secure and create a successful brand for the business:

Consistency in advertising: Brand advertising involves showing and emphasizing the unique points of the brand that competitors lack. These points must be repeatedly emphasized and announced so that they create a recovery value within your customer base. The public must be absolutely filled with these ads in order to regularly remember these brands.

Consumer Service: Human resources are a vital ingredient to the success of any business, so proper recruitment of sales personnel is essential. They must be sure of their position in the branding process. Every customer needs to be respected and

understood, and not being attentive or not
considering even a single customer can mean
massive losses to the business. Uncooperative
staff should be dismissed, because a
favorable customer response helps attract ten
more people.

Public perception: The treatment of a single
customer can spread very quickly by word of
mouth, and negative publicity jeopardizes
your business. While brand promotion, false
and illegitimate promises should not be
made. The purchase and billing process will
be simplified to ensure customer
convenience. Previous commitments must be
respected, punctually, to increase the
goodwill of the brand.

Use of technological advances: Denial of the

impact of the Internet on the promotion and marketing of businesses would be inappropriate. Internet inquiries from customers must be answered satisfactorily. The business must also be regularly updated and implemented with advanced technologies.

WE WISH YOU MANY SUCCESSFUL YOUNG ENTREPRENEURS!

Visit our author page on Amazon and get more MENTES LIBRES!

http://amazon.com/author/menteslibres

If you wish, you can leave a comment on this book by clicking on the following link so that we can continue to grow! Thank you very much for your purchase!

https://www.amazon.com/dp/B0827C6P62

www.ingramcontent.com/pod-product-compliance
Lightning Source LLC
Chambersburg PA
CBHW070855070326
40690CB00009B/1846